Cards with pips of flowers, fruits, birds, and animals. Middle of the seventeenth century.

013 014 015 016 017 018 019 020 021

Cards with symbols, of Parisian manufacture, published in the middle of the seventeenth century.

ROY DE DENIER ·
022

ROY DE BASTONS
023

ROY · DESPEE
024

ROY DE COVPPES ·
025

ROYNE · DE COVPES
026

CHEVALIER DE COVPES
027

VALE T DE COVPES
028

I · NOBLET · AVFAV
BOVR · St GERMAIN
029

IEAN NOBLET DMT AVFAVBOVRS t GERMAIN
030

Cards with Spanish suits, Paris, mid-eighteenth century.   3

031

032

033   034   035

Tarot cards supposedly owned by Charles VI.
031. The Emperor. 032. Strength. 033. Temperance. 034. The Jack of Swords. 035. Justice.

Deck of cards of the Revolutionary period, 1792.

Deck of cards designed by Houbigant, ca. 1818.

060   061   062

063   064   065

066   067   068

German double-headed picture cards, ca. 1860.

069 — LE BATELEVR · I ·

070 — LE CHARIOT VII

071 — LER MITE IX

072 — IVSTTICE VIII

073 — L'ESTOILLE · XVII ·

074 — LA LUNE XVIII

French tarot cards executed in the seventeenth century by an unknown Parisian card manufacturer.

Deck of cards of the street cries of Paris, 1830–40.

Picture cards of the kings and queens from "Deck of Cards for a Joke,"
each representing a paper published during the Second Restoration.

Deck of cards of questions and answers, Revolutionary era.

Deck of cards of "The Dowry or the Game of the Bride," (1820–30).

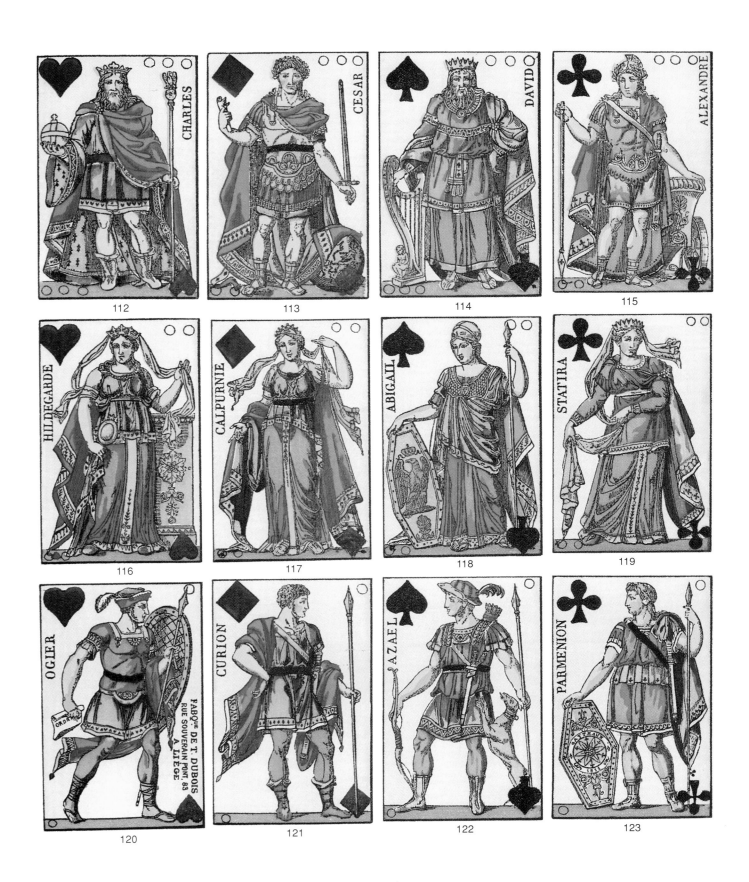

Deck of cards, Liège, 1811.

124   125   126   127

128   129   130   131

132   133   134   135

Deck of cards for fortune-telling, executed during the Restoration.

Deck of cards, published by Robert Passerel, Paris, 1622.

Jacks from Revolutionary decks of cards, Paris and Reims.

153   154   155

156   157   158

159   160   161

Cards from an *alluette* deck, Nantes, beginning of the nineteenth century.

Deck of cards of the Revolutionary period, Paris, 1792.

GRAND HONNEUR.	RENTIER.	HOMME DE COMMERCE.	HOMME DE ROBE
174	175	176	177
TENDRESSE.	AMOUR D'ARGENT.	MÉCHANTE FEMME.	FEMME VEUVE.
178	179	180	181
GÉNÉROSITÉ.	FLATTEUR	UN MILITAIRE.	MESSAGER
182	183	184	185

"The Little Sorcerer," a fortune-telling game, beginning of the nineteenth century.

20   Deck of cards of the rulers of Europe, end of the Second Empire.

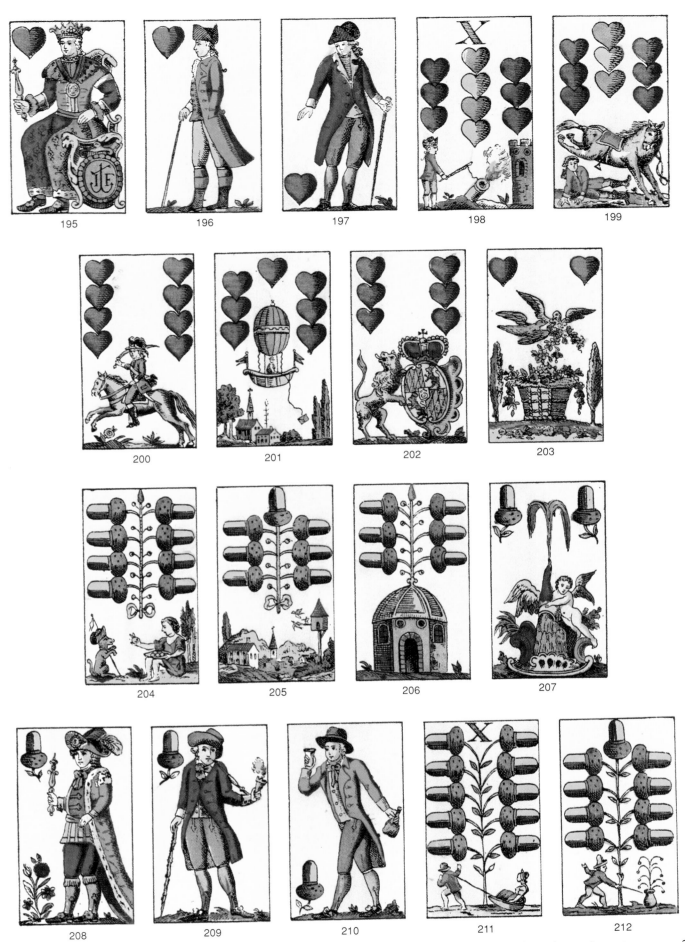

Children's game with German suits, featuring the depiction of a balloon, Munich, eighteenth century.

Duplication of Jaume and Dugourc's deck, Nantes, late eighteenth century.

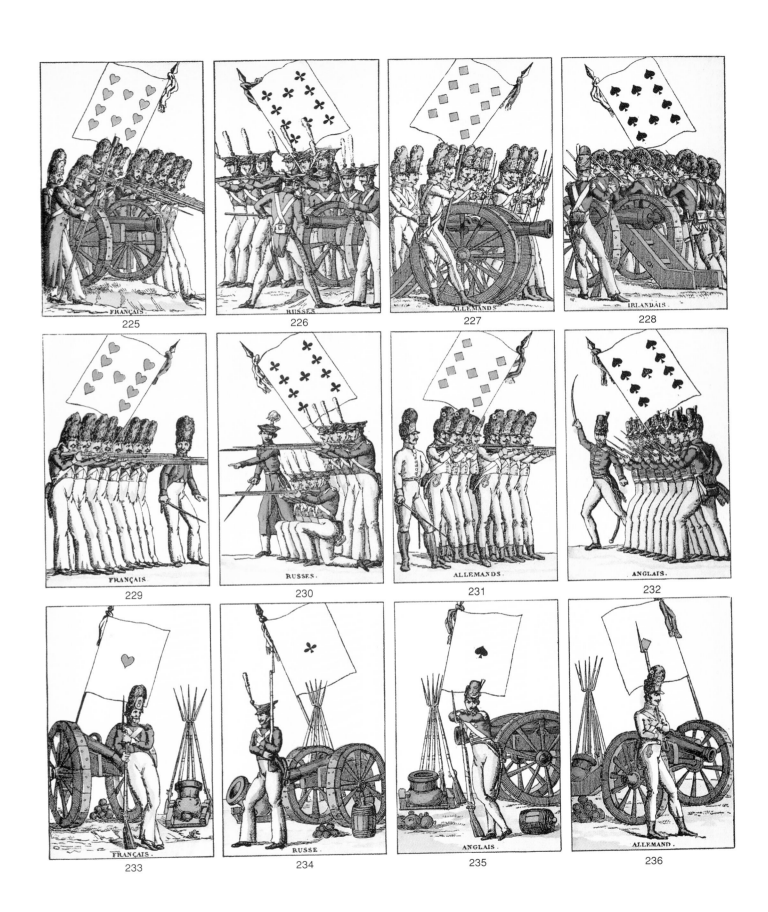

Number cards from the game of the flags, after a deck published during the Restoration.

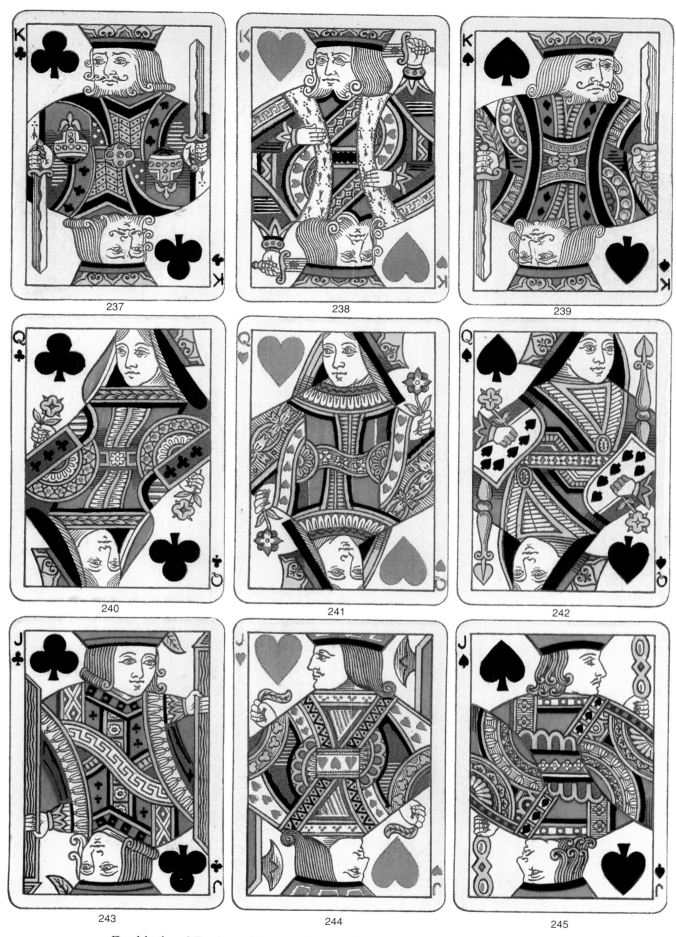

237 238 239
240 241 242
243 244 245

24   Double-faced English picture cards, London, end of the nineteenth century.

Tarot deck, alleged to have belonged to Charles VI, fifteenth century.
246. The Fool. 247. The Knave. 248. The Emperor. 249. The Pope. 250. The Lovers. 251. Fortune.

Round deck of cards engraved in Cologne, ca. 1477.

Parisian deck of cards published by Jean Trioullier, 1681–1703.

Cards from a Parisian deck, second half of the seventeenth century.

Picture cards in the Dauphiné style, published by Jehan Genevoy, Lyons, 1591–97.

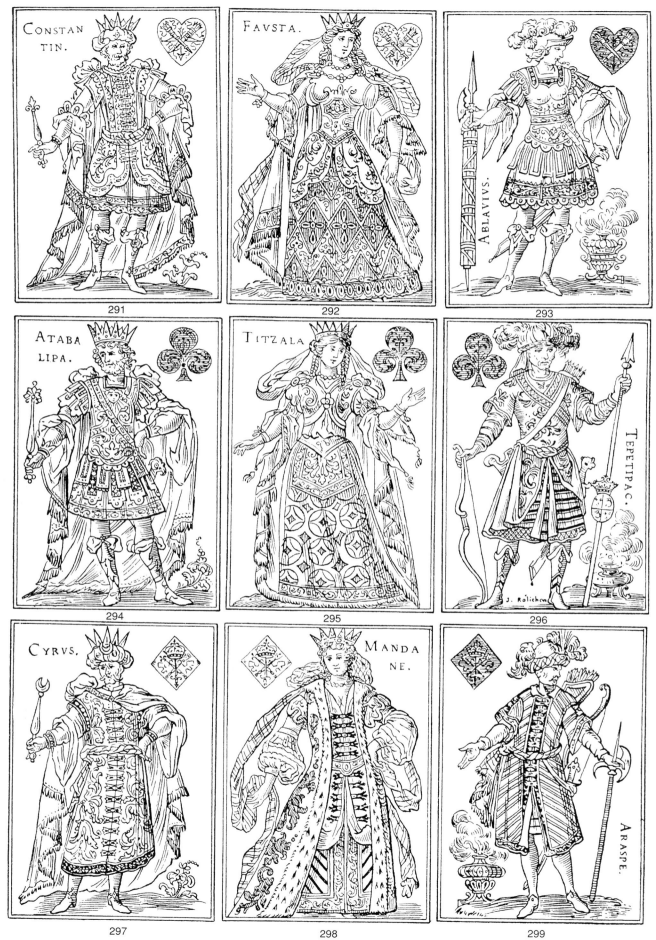

CONSTAN TIN.

FAVSTA.

ABLAVIVS.

291

292

293

ATABA LIPA.

TITZALA

TEPETIPAC.

294

295

296

CYRVS.

MANDA NE.

ARASPE.

J. Rolichon

297

298

299

Cards from a fantasy deck, published by Jean Rolichon, Lyons, 1660–74.

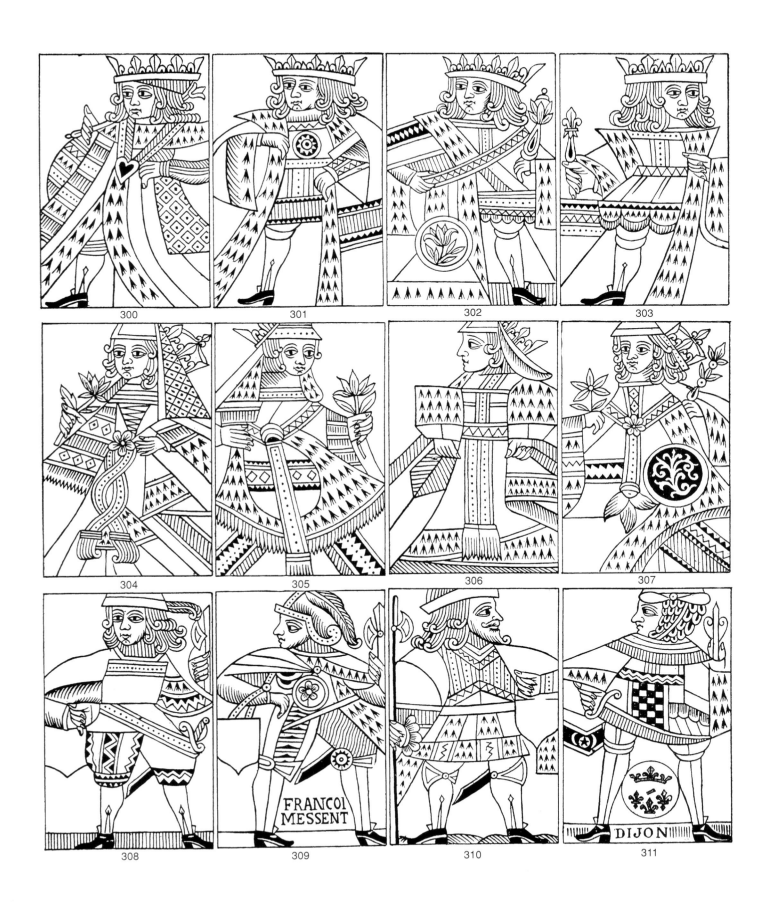

Picture cards in the Burgundian style, ca. 1752.

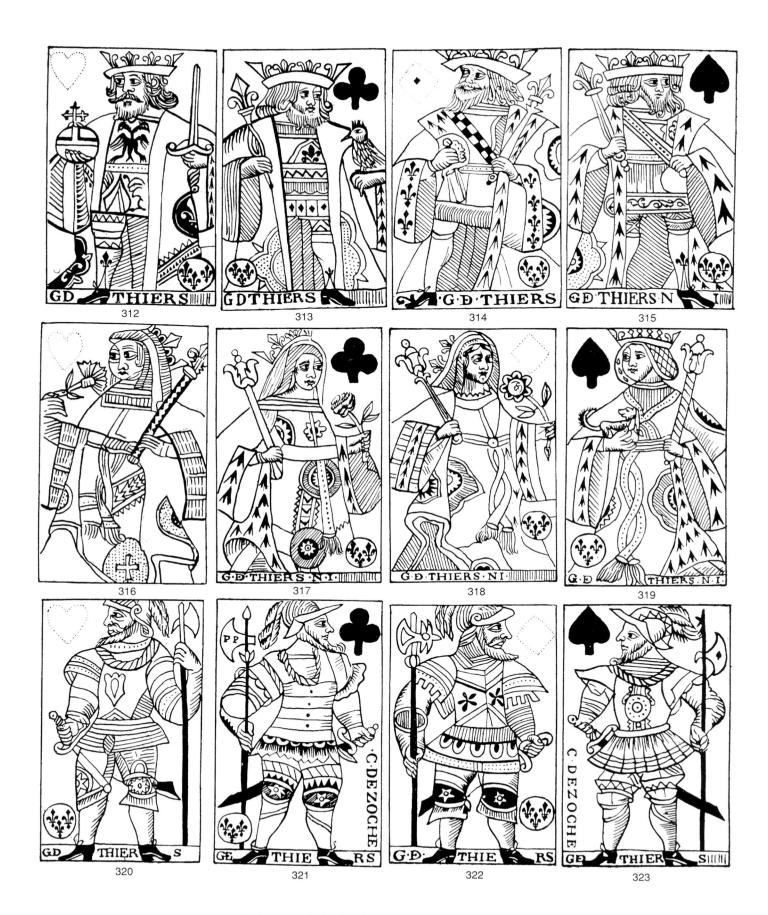

Picture cards in the Auvergne style, ca. 1701–02.

324 325 326 327

328 329 330 331

332 333 334 335

Picture cards in the Guyenne style, ca. 1746.

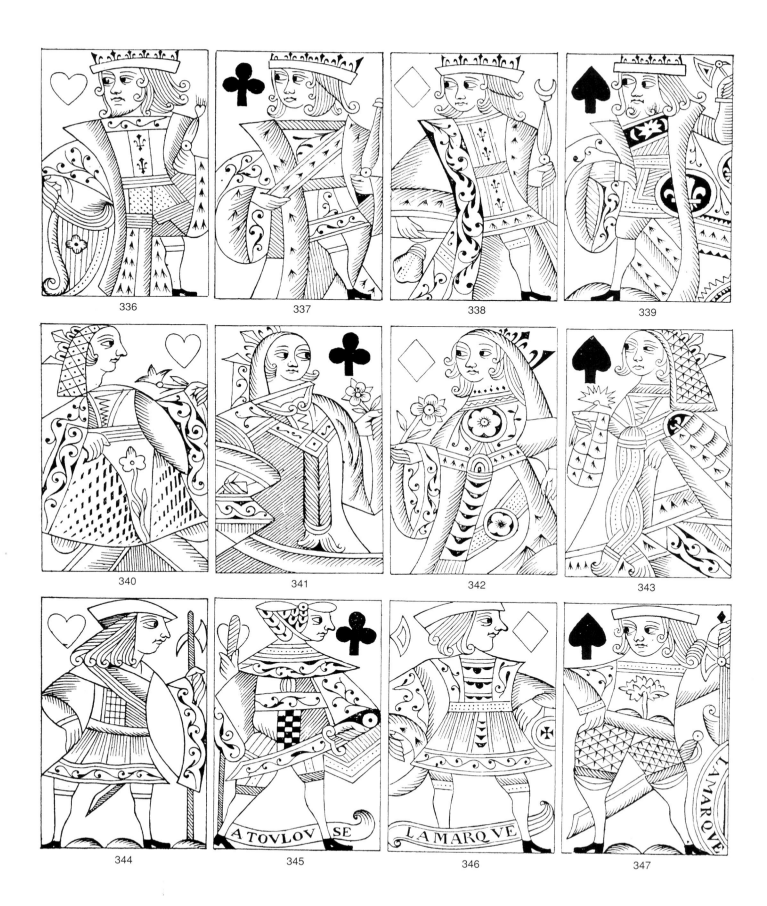

336 337 338 339

340 341 342 343

344 345 346 347

Picture cards in the Languedoc style, published by Lamarque, ca. 1720.

Cards from a Revolutionary deck, published by Pinaut, Paris.

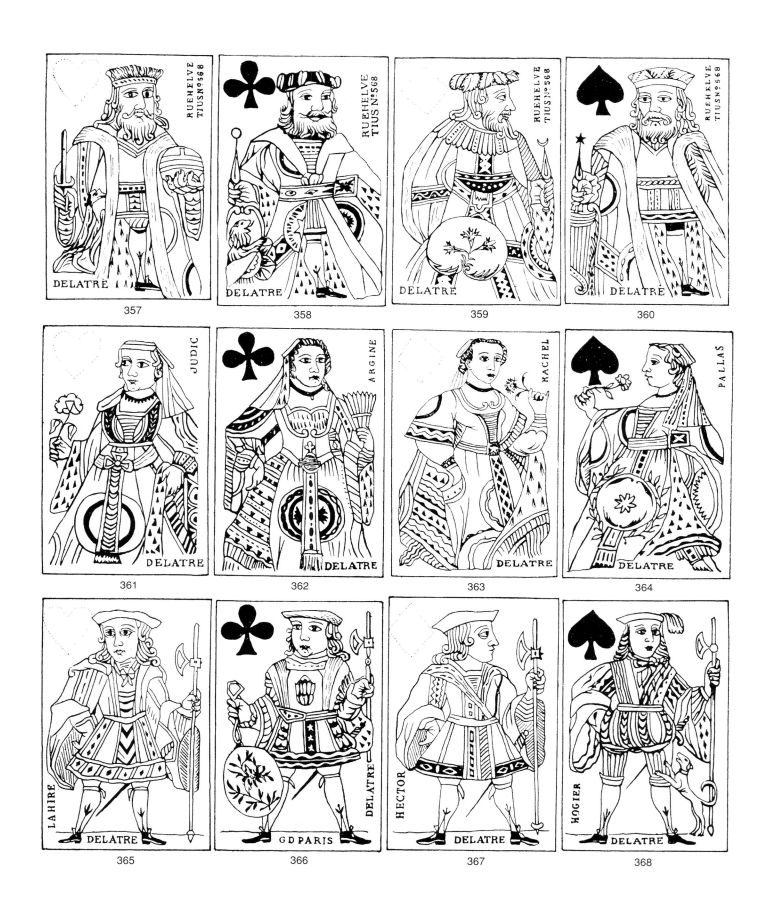

Picture cards in the Parisian style turned into a Revolutionary pack by Delâtre, Paris.

Imperial deck engraved by Andrieu, after sketches by David, 1808–10.

Picture cards in the official style, 1816.

Cards from the recasting of the deck created by Houbigant, published by Mme. Dambrin, ca. 1818.

405   406   407

408   409   410

411   412   413

Republican deck created by Bertrand, ca. 1872, published by Maison Leclaire, Paris.

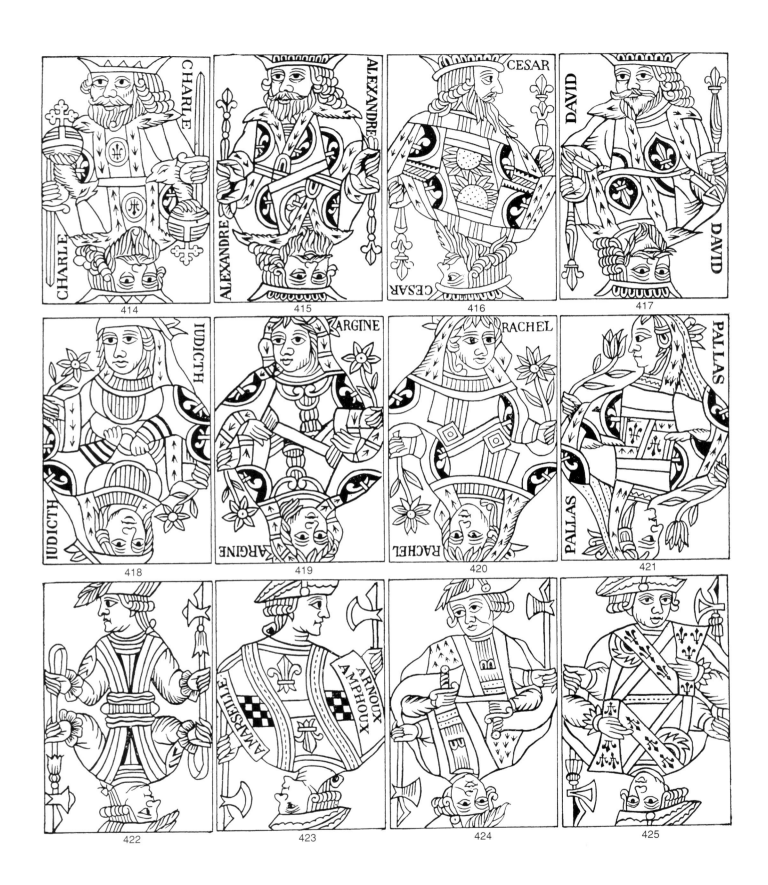

Double-headed picture cards, published by Maison Arnoux et Amphoux, Marseilles, 1806.

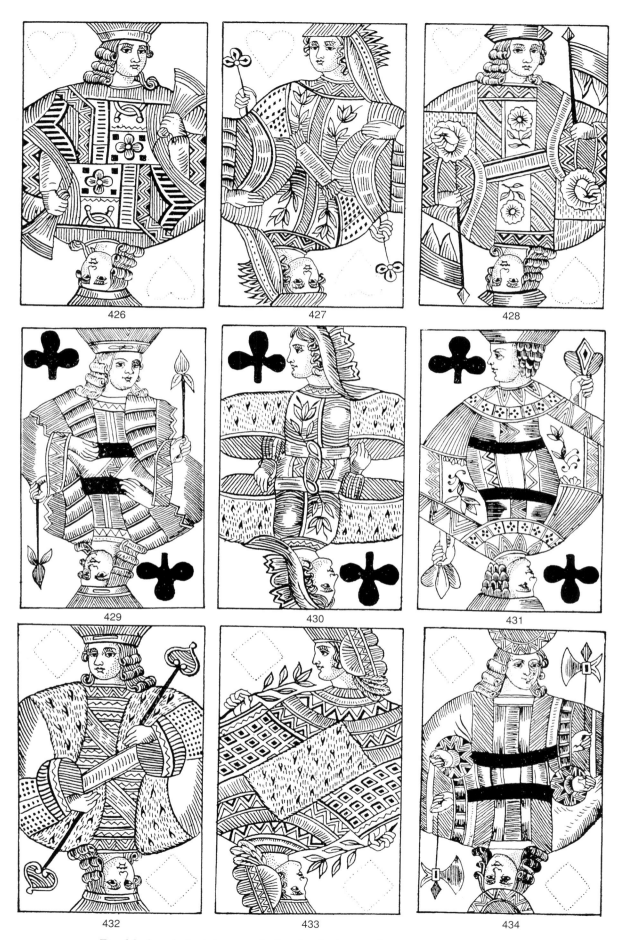

426 427 428

429 430 431

432 433 434

Double-headed picture cards for the Swiss market, nineteenth century.

Trumps from a tarot deck, eighteenth century.

446 447 448
449 450 451
452 453 454

Educational deck by Murner, sixteenth century.

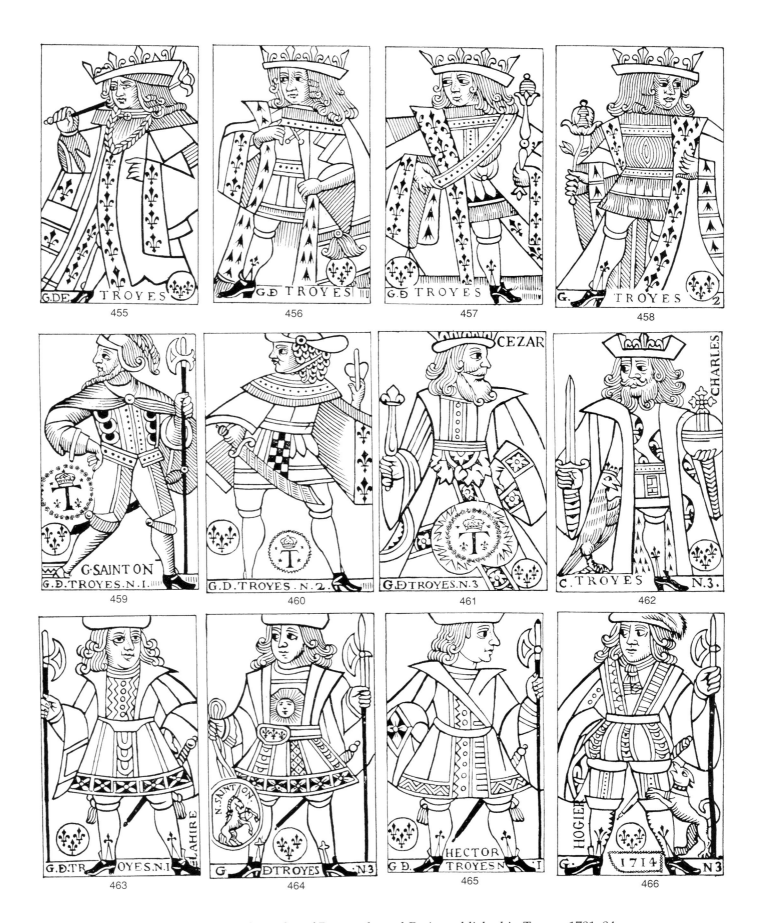

Picture cards in the styles of Burgundy and Paris, published in Troyes, 1701–04.

467   468   469

470   471   472

French cards drawn and painted by hand, end of the fifteenth century.

473 474 475 476

477 478 479 480

481 482 483 484

Pirated picture cards in the Provence style, eighteenth century.

Deck of royal emblematic figures, created in honor of the accession of
Louis XVIII, published by Bayard, Paris, 1816.